PIANO/VOCAL/GUITAR

# EMELI SANDÉ

## OUR VERSION OF EVENTS

ISBN 978-1-4803-5359-6

## HAL•LEONARD®
### CORPORATION

7777 W. BLUEMOUND RD. P.O. BOX 13819 MILWAUKEE, WI 53213

For all works contained herein:
Unauthorized copying, arranging, adapting, recording, Internet posting, public performance,
or other distribution of the printed music in this publication is an infringement of copyright.
Infringers are liable under the law.

In Australia Contact:
**Hal Leonard Australia Pty. Ltd.**
4 Lentara Court
Cheltenham, Victoria, 3192 Australia
Email: ausadmin@halleonard.com.au

Visit Hal Leonard Online at
**www.halleonard.com**

# HEAVEN

Words and Music by EMELI SANDÉ,
SHAHID KHAN, MICHAEL SPENCER,
HUGO CHEGWIN and HARRY CRAZE

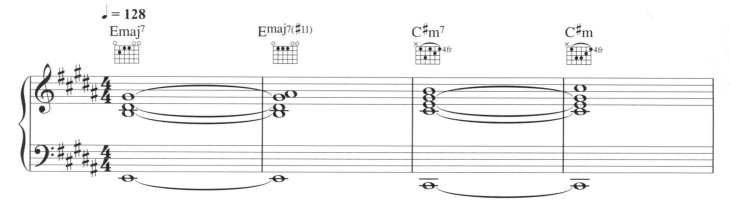

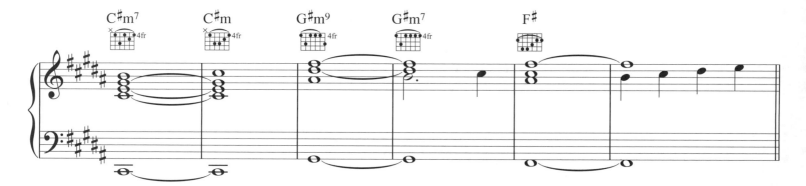

1. Will you re-cog-nise me in the flash-ing lights?____
2. Will you re-cog-nise me when I'm steal-ing from the poor?__

© 2011, 2012 STELLAR SONGS LTD., SONY/ATV MUSIC PUBLISHING UK LIMITED and NAUGHTY WORDS LIMITED
All Rights for STELLAR SONGS LTD. in the U.S. and Canada Controlled and Administered by EMI BLACKWOOD MUSIC INC.
All Rights for SONY/ATV MUSIC PUBLISHING UK LIMITED and NAUGHTY WORDS LIMITED Administered by SONY/ATV MUSIC PUBLISHING LLC, 8 Music Square West, Nashville, TN 37203
All Rights Reserved   International Copyright Secured   Used by Permission

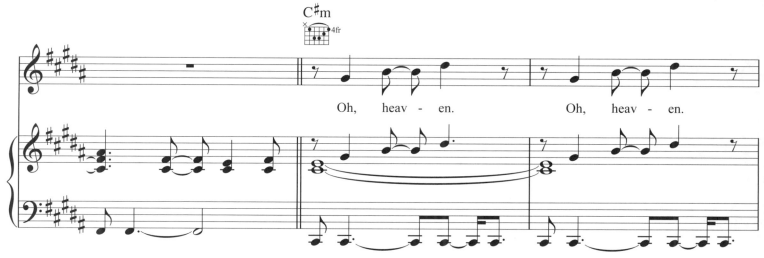

try but al-ways break. 'Cause the day al-ways lasts__ too long.__ Then I'm gone.

__ Then I'm gone.__ Then I'm gone.__ Then I'm__ gone. Then I'm gone.__

**1.**

__ Then I'm gone.__ Then I'm gone.__ Then I'm gone.

**2.**

Then I'm gone.__ Then I'm__ gone.__

# MY KIND OF LOVE

Words and Music by EMELI SANDÉ,
EMILE HAYNIE and DANIEL TANNENBAUM

1. I can't buy your love. Don't e-ven wan-na try.
2. You won't see me at the par-ties, I guess I'm just no fun.

Some-times the truth won't make you hap-py, still I'm not gon-na lie.
I won't be turn-ing up the ra-di-o sing-ing ba-by you're the one.

But don't ev-er ques-tion if my heart beats on-ly for you.

© 2012 STELLAR SONGS LTD., UNIVERSAL MUSIC CORP., HEAVYCRATE PUBLISHING and DANIKEYZ PRODUCTIONS
All Rights for STELLAR SONGS LTD. in the U.S. and Canada Controlled and Administered by EMI Blackwood Music Inc.
All Rights for HEAVYCRATE PUBLISHING Controlled and Administered by UNIVERSAL MUSIC CORP.
All Rights for DANIKEYZ PRODUCTIONS Controlled and Administered by SONGS OF UNIVERSAL, INC.
All Rights Reserved    International Copyright Secured    Used by Permission

It beats on - ly for you.

Know I'm far___ from per - fect, noth - in' like your en - tou - rage.___
I know some-times I___ get an - gry and I say what I don't mean.___

___ I can't grant___ you an - y wish - es,___ I won't prom - ise you___ the stars.
___ I know I keep my heart___ pro - tect - ed,___ far a - way from my___ sleeve.

But don't ev - er ques - tion if my heart beats on - ly for you.

It beats on - ly for you. 'Cause when you've

giv - en up,___ when no mat - ter what___ you do___ it's nev - er

good e - nough,___ when you nev - er thought___ that it could ev - er

get this tough,_____ that's when you feel my kind___ of___ love.___

'Cause when you've

giv-en up,___ when no mat-ter what__ you do__ it's nev-er

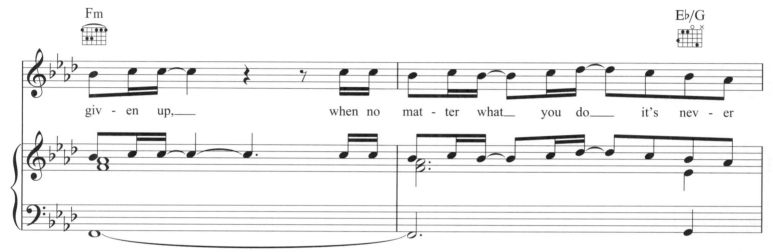

good e-nough,___ when you nev-er thought__ that it could ev-er

get this tough,___ that's when you feel my kind__ of__ love.___

# WHERE I SLEEP

Words and Music by EMELI SANDÉ
and SHAHID KHAN

© 2012 STELLAR SONGS LTD. and SONY/ATV MUSIC PUBLISHING UK LIMITED
All Rights for STELLAR SONGS LTD. in the U.S. and Canada Controlled and Administered by EMI BLACKWOOD MUSIC INC.
All Rights for SONY/ATV MUSIC PUBLISHING UK LIMITED Administered by SONY/ATV MUSIC PUBLISHING LLC, 8 Music Square West, Nashville, TN 37203
All Rights Reserved   International Copyright Secured   Used by Permission

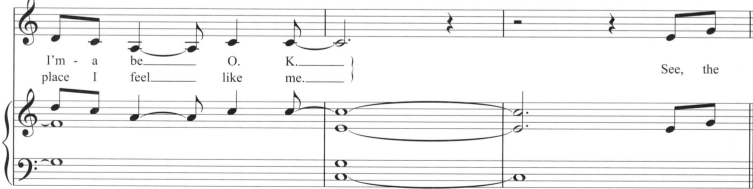

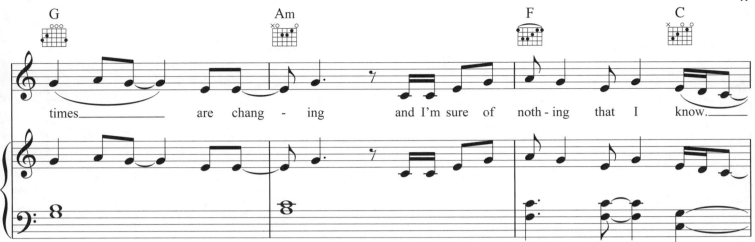

times_____ are chang - ing and I'm sure of noth-ing that I know._____

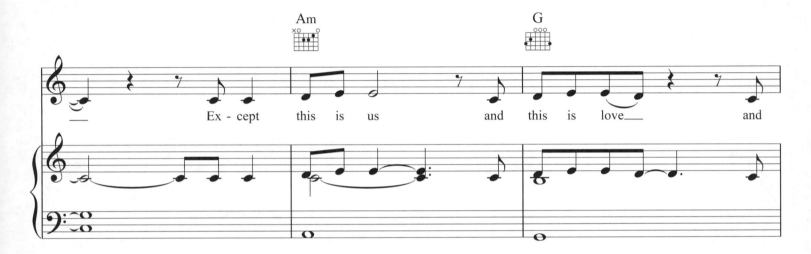

_____ Ex - cept this is us and this is love_____ and

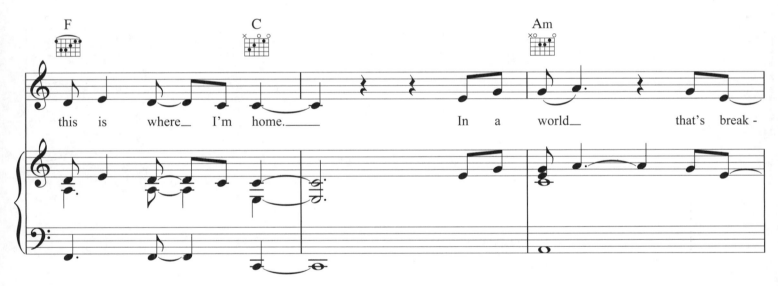

this is where_ I'm home._____ In a world_ that's break -

- ing, where noth - ing is_____ for keeps._____ Oh,

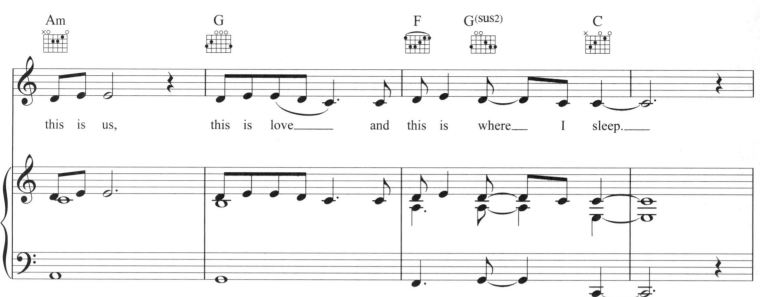

this is us, this is love_____ and this is where__ I sleep.__

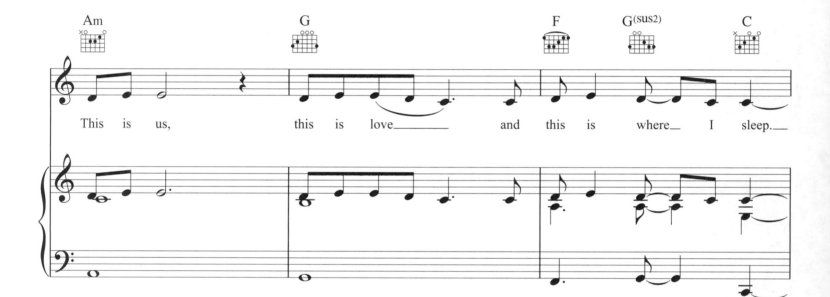

This is us, this is love_____ and this is where__ I sleep.__

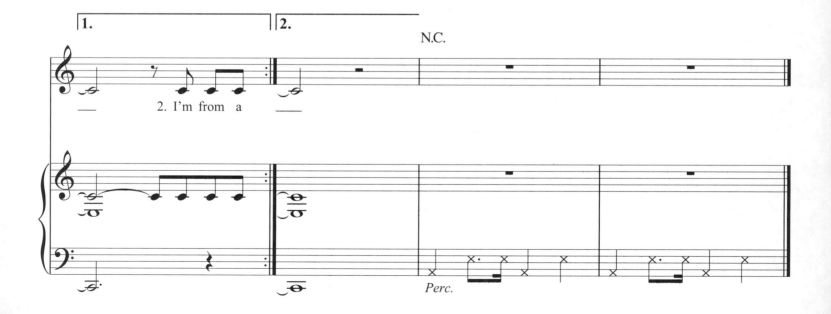

**1.** **2.**

N.C.

2. I'm from a

# MOUNTAINS

Words and Music by EMELI SANDÉ,
SHAHID KHAN, MUSTAFA OMER,
JAMES MURRAY and LUKE JUBY

1. He said I'm gon-na have a bed with lots of pil-lows.
2. I'd nev-er work these hours if I did-n't love you.

And that we're gon-na build a house with lots of win-dows.
My hands are al-ways red and sun-shine I sleep through.

© 2012 STELLAR SONGS LTD., SONY/ATV MUSIC PUBLISHING UK LIMITED and PEERMUSIC (UK) LTD.
All Rights for STELLAR SONGS LTD. in the U.S. and Canada Controlled and Administered by EMI BLACKWOOD MUSIC INC.
All Rights for SONY/ATV MUSIC PUBLISHING UK LIMITED Administered by SONY/ATV MUSIC PUBLISHING LLC, 8 Music Square West, Nashville, TN 37203
All Rights Reserved   International Copyright Secured   Used by Permission

And when we have the kids we'll tell them to re-
If you say we're gon-na move some-where with neigh-bours less cra-

mind we___
-zy.___

of where we were and
You know I'm gon-na

how so we nev-er get la - zy.___ }
be there 'cause I trust my ba - by.___ }

*

Yeah,___ we'll

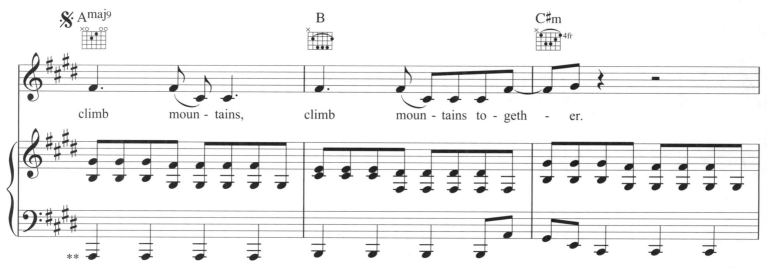

climb moun - tains, climb moun - tains to - geth - er.

Yeah,____ we'll climb moun - tains, climb moun - tains to - geth-

*2° Instrumental ad lib.*

- er. Yeah,____ we'll climb moun - tains, climb moun - tains to - geth-

- er.

# CLOWN

Words and Music by EMELI SANDÉ,
SHAHID KHAN and GRANT MITCHELL

1. I guess it's fun-ni-er from where you're stand-ing,___

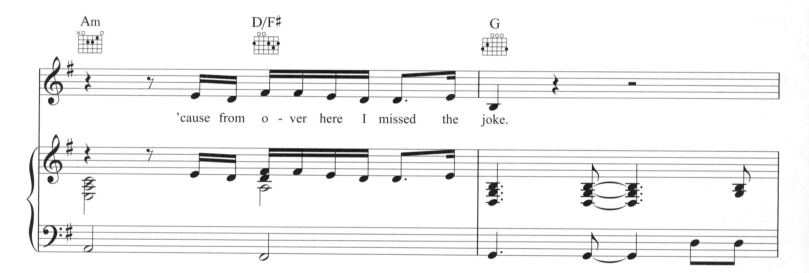

'cause from o-ver here I missed the joke.

Clear the way for my crash land-ing.___ I've done it a-gain,___

© 2012 STELLAR SONGS LTD., SONY/ATV MUSIC PUBLISHING UK LIMITED and IQ MUSIC LTD.
All Rights for STELLAR SONGS LTD. in the U.S. and Canada Controlled and Administered by EMI BLACKWOOD MUSIC INC.
All Rights for SONY/ATV MUSIC PUBLISHING UK LIMITED Administered by SONY/ATV MUSIC PUBLISHING LLC, 8 Music Square West, Nashville, TN 37203
All Rights Reserved   International Copyright Secured   Used by Permission

make-up on___ my face.___ But there's no way you can feel___ it from so

far a - way.___ I'll be your

*D.S. al Coda*

*Coda*

cir - cus, cir - cus. 'Round in cir - cles. I'm sell - ing out___ to - night.

# DADDY

Words and Music by EMELI SANDÉ,
SHAHID KHAN, MUSTAFA OMER,
JAMES MURRAY and GRANT MITCHELL

1. He's out your sys - tem, yeah, it took you a while.
2. He kissed you on the lips and o - pened your eyes.

You got your fam -'ly back and you got your smile. And you prom - ised your sis - ter that you'd
You had to catch your breath, got such a sur - prise. And you al - most for - got how it

nev - er go back a - gain.
feels to live in his light.

© 2012 STELLAR SONGS LTD., SONY/ATV MUSIC PUBLISHING UK LIMITED and IQ MUSIC LTD.
All Rights for STELLAR SONGS LTD. in the U.S. and Canada Controlled and Administered by EMI BLACKWOOD MUSIC INC.
All Rights for SONY/ATV MUSIC PUBLISHING UK LIMITED Administered by SONY/ATV MUSIC PUBLISHING LLC, 8 Music Square West, Nashville, TN 37203
All Rights Reserved   International Copyright Secured   Used by Permission

# MAYBE

Words and Music by EMELI SANDÉ,
PAUL HERMAN and ASHTON MILLARD

1. When we first__ moved in__ to-geth-er could-n't keep__ hands off__ each oth-
2. We broke up__ last Sun-day night__ keep on think-ing 'bout the fight.__

© 2012 STELLAR SONGS LTD., PAUL HERMAN PUBLISHING DESIGNEE and ASHTON MILLARD PUBLISHING DESIGNEE
All Rights for STELLAR SONGS LTD. in the U.S. and Canada Controlled and Administered by EMI BLACKWOOD MUSIC INC.
All Rights Reserved   International Copyright Secured   Used by Permission

But I don't wan-na give up what we've got.
But I don't wan-na give up yet be-cause...

May-be you could stay_ a bit long-er, I could try_ a bit hard-er. We could make_ this

work. But may-be we should stop_ pre-tend-ing. We both know_ we're
Both of us_ are

hurt-ing. May-be it's time_ to go. go.

⊕ *Coda*

go._____ May - be it's time__ to go.

*Vocal ad lib. on repeat*

B♭maj7

May - be we could make this work._____

1. May-be it's time__ to

2. May-be it's time__ to go.

F

# SUITCASE

Words and Music by EMELI SANDÉ,
SHAHID KHAN, BENJAMIN HARRISON
and LUKE JUBY

1. Did-n't see it com - - ing, no kind of warn - ing.
2. What changed so quick - ly? An - swer me! If you

I can't work out what I've done wrong.
must kill me at least please tell me why.

© 2012 STELLAR SONGS LTD., SONY/ATV MUSIC PUBLISHING UK LIMITED, WB MUSIC CORP., ROC INTERNATIONAL PUBLISHING and PEERMUSIC (UK) LTD.
All Rights for STELLAR SONGS LTD. in the U.S. and Canada Controlled and Administered by EMI BLACKWOOD MUSIC INC.
All Rights for SONY/ATV MUSIC PUBLISHING UK LIMITED Administered by SONY/ATV MUSIC PUBLISHING LLC, 8 Music Square West, Nashville, TN 37203
All Rights Reserved   International Copyright Secured   Used by Permission

His    clothes  are   miss  -  ing          but his key's still here.
He     says "don't touch  me,              get out the way."       Will

Please some-bod-y  tell me what's go  -  ing  on.
some  -  one  tell me what's go - ing  on        to - night?        My ba-by's got a

suit  -  case.     He's tell - ing me it's too    late.       But

don't no - bod - y,  please don't ask___  me  why._____     'Cause all I did was

*D.S. al Coda*

heart 'cause he won't look at me an - y - more.___ My ba - by's got a

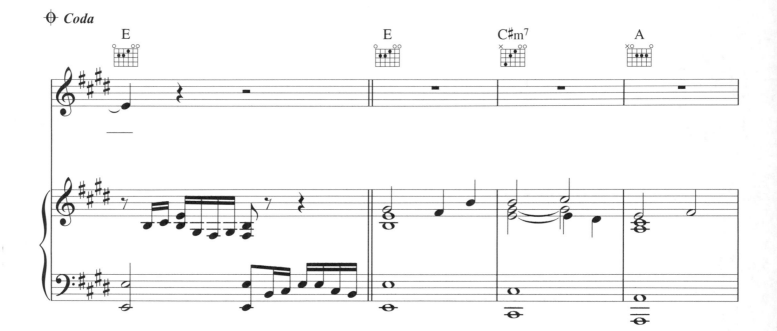

**Coda**

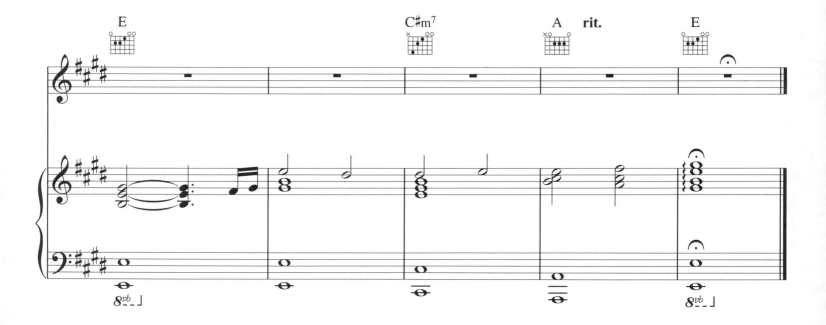

**rit.**

# BREAKING THE LAW

Words and Music by EMELI SANDÉ,
SHAHID KHAN and BENJAMIN HARRISON

© 2012 STELLAR SONGS LTD., SONY/ATV MUSIC PUBLISHING UK LIMITED, WB MUSIC CORP. and ROC INTERNATIONAL PUBLISHING
All Rights for STELLAR SONGS LTD. in the U.S. and Canada Controlled and Administered by EMI BLACKWOOD MUSIC INC.
All Rights for SONY/ATV MUSIC PUBLISHING UK LIMITED Administered by SONY/ATV MUSIC PUBLISHING LLC, 8 Music Square West, Nashville, TN 37203
All Rights Reserved   International Copyright Secured   Used by Permission

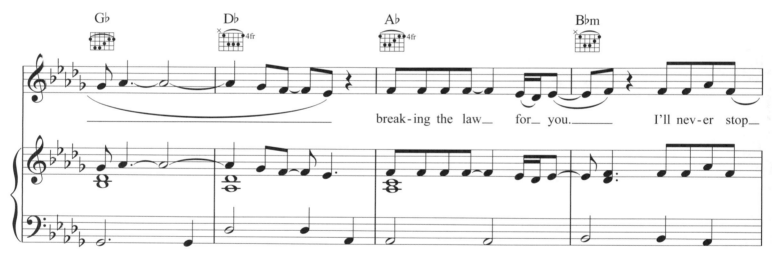

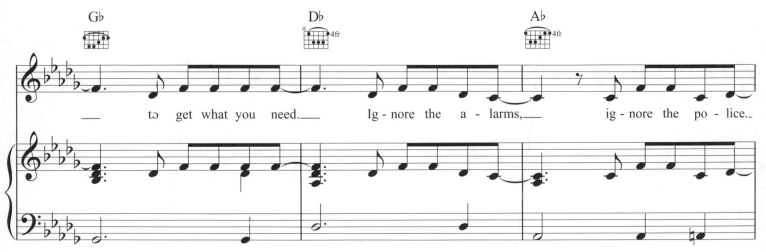

to get what you need.___ Ig - nore the a - larms,___ ig - nore the po - lice.__

I'll nev - er stop___

break - ing the law___ for___ you.___ 2. When you're tak -___ I'll nev - er stop___

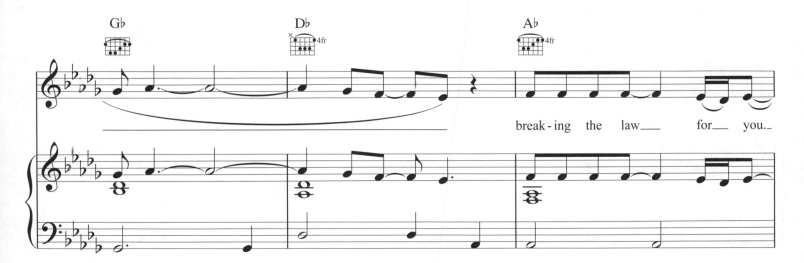

break - ing the law___ for___ you.__

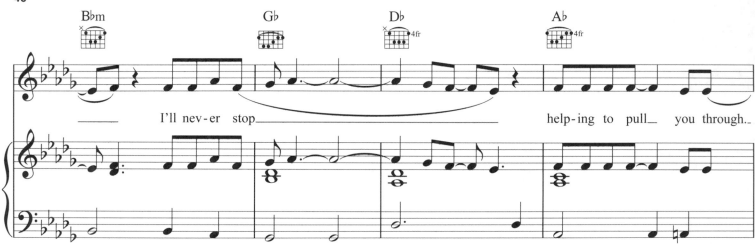

I'll nev-er stop_____ help-ing to pull\_\_ you through..

\_\_ What-ev-er it takes\_\_ to get what you need.\_\_ Ig-nore the a-larms,\_\_ ig-nore the po-lice..

\_\_ I'll nev-er stop_____ break-ing the law\_\_ for\_\_ you..

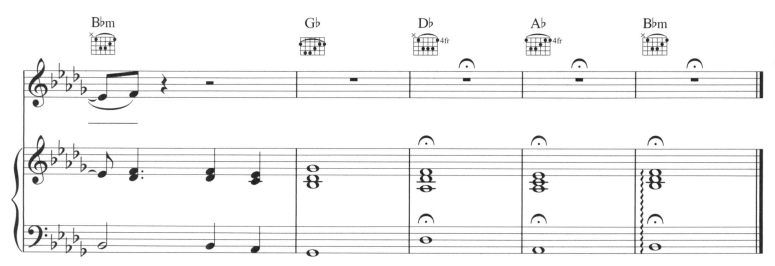

# NEXT TO ME

Words and Music by EMELI SANDÉ,
HARRY CRAZE, HUGO CHEGWIN
and ANUP PAUL

1. You won't find__ him drink-ing un-der ta-bles,
2. You won't find__ him try'n'__ to change__ the dev-il

roll-ing__ dice__ and stay-ing out__ till three.
for mon-ey, fame,__ for pow-er, out__ of greed.

© 2012 STELLAR SONGS LTD., SONY/ATV MUSIC PUBLISHING UK LIMITED, NAUGHTY WORDS LIMITED and ANUP PAUL PUBLISHING DESIGNEE
All Rights for STELLAR SONGS LTD. in the U.S. and Canada Controlled and Administered by EMI BLACKWOOD MUSIC INC.
All Rights for SONY/ATV MUSIC PUBLISHING UK LIMITED and NAUGHTY WORDS LIMITED Administered by SONY/ATV MUSIC PUBLISHING LLC, 8 Music Square West, Nashville, TN 37203
All Rights Reserved   International Copyright Secured   Used by Permission

You won't ev - er find__ him be__ un - faith - ful. You will find__
You won't ev - er find__ him where__ the rest__ go. You will find__

**1.**
**2.**

__ him, you'll find__ him next to me.
__ him, you'll find__ him next to me. Next to me,__

ooh.__ Next to me,__ ooh.__

Next to me,__ ooh.__

You will find___ him, you'll find___ him next to me.___ 3. When the

mon - ey's___ spent and all___ my friends have van - ished and I can't
(4.) skies are grey___ and all___ the doors___ are clos - ing and the

seem to find___ no help or love___ for free.___
ris - ing pres - sure makes it hard___ to breathe.___ When all I

I know there's no need___ for me___ to pan - ic. 'Cause I'll find___
need's a hand to stop___ the tears___ from fall - ing. I will find___

# RIVER

Words and Music by EMELI SANDÉ
and SHAHID KHAN

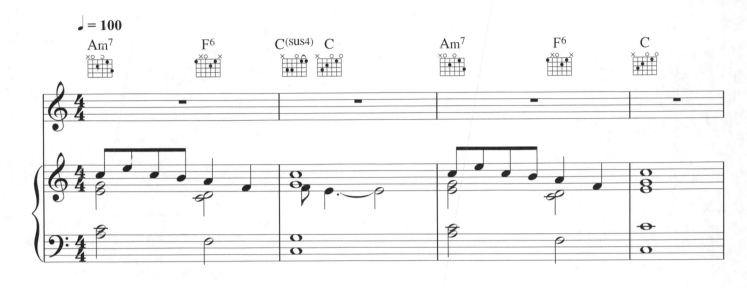

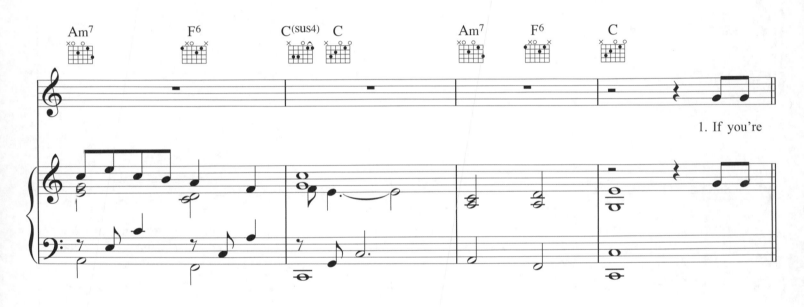

1. If you're

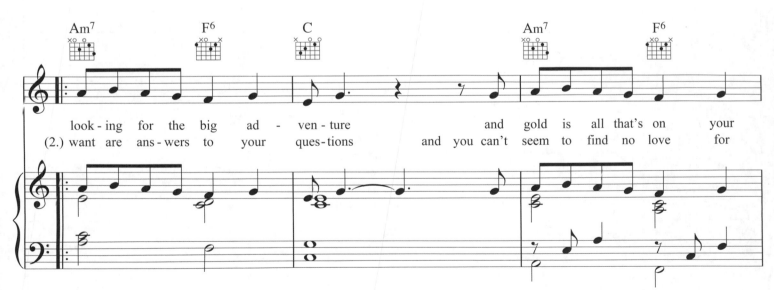

look- ing for the big ad - ven - ture and gold is all that's on your
(2.) want are ans - wers to your ques - tions and you can't seem to find no love for

© 2012 STELLAR SONGS LTD. and SONY/ATV MUSIC PUBLISHING UK LIMITED
All Rights for STELLAR SONGS LTD. in the U.S. and Canada Controlled and Administered by EMI BLACKWOOD MUSIC INC.
All Rights for SONY/ATV MUSIC PUBLISHING UK LIMITED Administered by SONY/ATV MUSIC PUBLISHING LLC, 8 Music Square West, Nashville, TN 37203
All Rights Reserved   International Copyright Secured   Used by Permission

# LIFETIME

Words and Music by EMELI SANDÉ,
SHAHID KHAN, STEVE MOSTYN,
GLYN AIKINS and LUKE JUBY

© 2012 STELLAR SONGS LTD., SONY/ATV MUSIC PUBLISHING UK LIMITED, OZMOD MUSIC, NANAS HANDS and PEERMUSIC (UK) LTD.
All Rights for STELLAR SONGS LTD. in the U.S. and Canada Controlled and Administered by EMI BLACKWOOD MUSIC INC.
All Rights for SONY/ATV MUSIC PUBLISHING UK LIMITED, OZMOD MUSIC and NANAS HANDS Administered by SONY/ATV MUSIC PUBLISHING LLC, 8 Music Square West, Nashville, TN 37203
All Rights Reserved   International Copyright Secured   Used by Permission

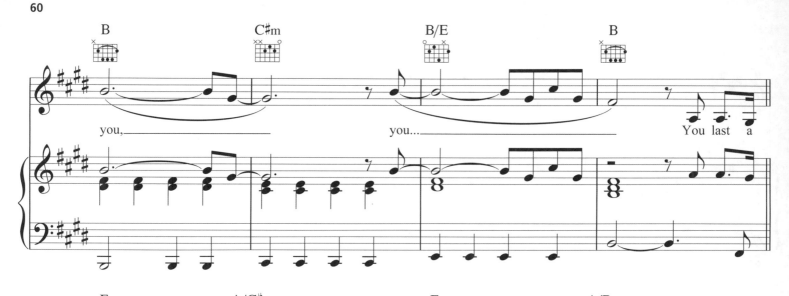

you,_____ you..._____ You last a

life-time.____ You last a life-time.

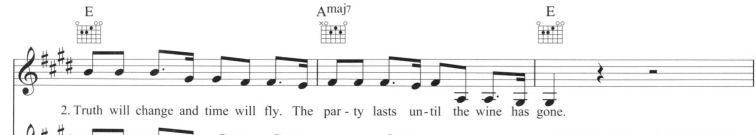

2. Truth will change and time will fly. The par-ty lasts un-til the wine has gone.

This time next week the ra-di-o_____ will change it's mind_ and play a dif-f'rent

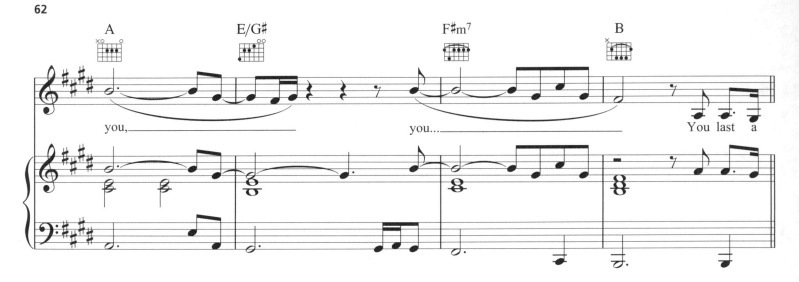

you,_____ you..._____ You last a

life - time._____ You last a life - time.

Hey____ love,____ can we dance_____ to - geth - er?

Since I found you feels like time____ don't mat - ter. Hey__ love,__ now I

feel\_\_\_\_ much bet - ter. You've shown me for - ev - - er.\_\_\_ See

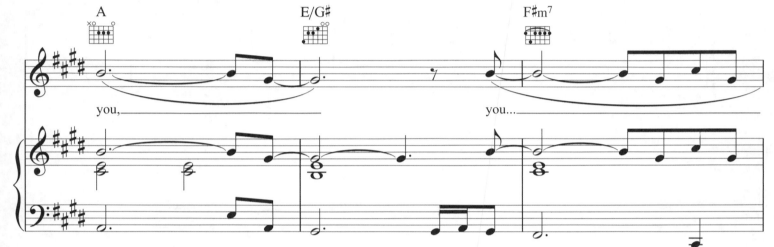

you,_____ you..._____

\_\_ You last a life - time.\_\_\_ You last a

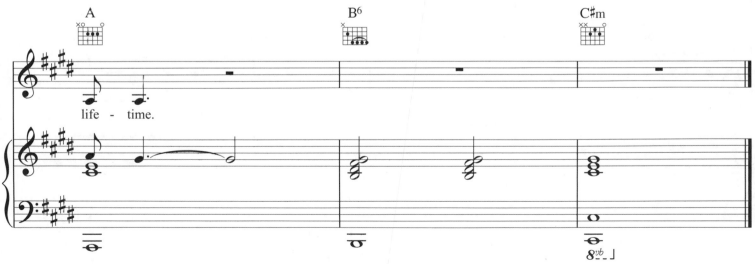

life - time.

# HOPE

Words and Music by EMELI SANDÉ
and ALICIA KEYS

1. I hope that the world stops rain-ing,_____ stops
(2.) hope we start see-ing for-ev-er in-stead of

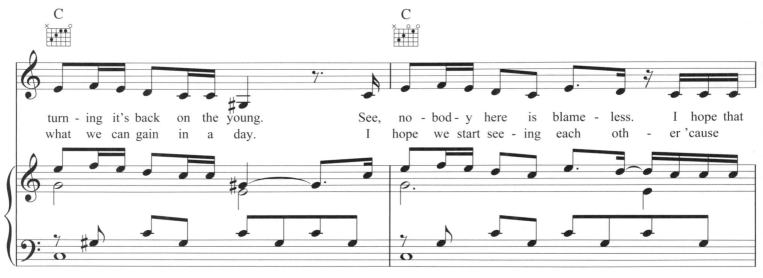

turn-ing it's back on the young. See, no-bod-y here is blame-less. I hope that
what we can gain in a day. I hope we start see-ing each oth-er 'cause

we can fix all that we've done. I real-ly hope Mar-tin can see this. I
don't we all bleed the same? I real-ly hope some-one can hear me, that a

© 2012 STELLAR SONGS LTD., EMI APRIL MUSIC INC. and LELLOW PRODUCTIONS
All Rights for STELLAR SONGS LTD. in the U.S. and Canada Controlled and Administered by EMI BLACKWOOD MUSIC INC.
All Rights for LELLOW PRODUCTIONS Controlled and Administered by EMI APRIL MUSIC INC.
All Rights Reserved   International Copyright Secured   Used by Permission

hope that we still have a dream. I'm hop-ing that change is-n't hope-less.___ I'm
child does-n't bear the weight of a gun. Hope I've found a voice with-in me,___ to

hop-ing to start it with me.___ I just hope___ I'm not the on-ly
scream at the top of my lungs.___ I just hope___ I'm not the on-ly

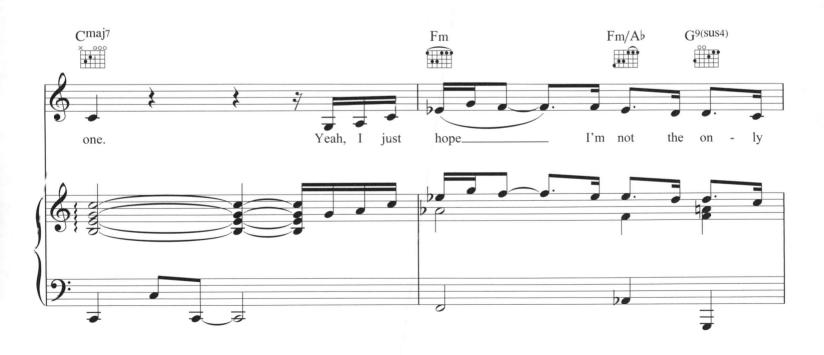

one. Yeah, I just hope___ I'm not the on-ly

seems that dreams are all that we've got left. Ooh. I

hope we still have a heart - beat. I hope we don't turn to stone. At

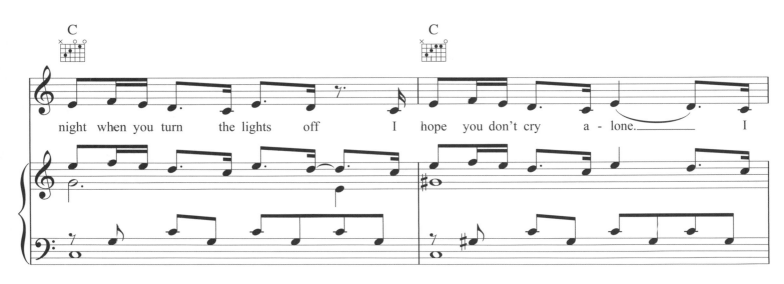

night when you turn the lights off I hope you don't cry a - lone._____ I

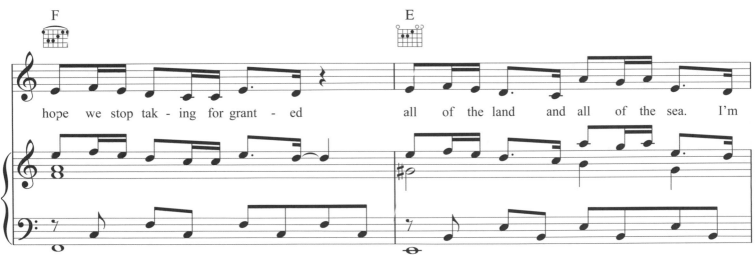

hope we stop tak - ing for grant - ed all of the land and all of the sea. I'm

# TIGER

Words and Music by EMELI SANDÉ
and SHAHID KHAN

1. Drop all the pills doc tor told us to take. They say we're dream-in' but I swear we're a-wake. When
2. You'll build a plane and I'll build a boat. If we drop all the sil-ver I swear we can float. Was-n't

-ev-er you leave all the col-ours fade.__ So I'm here hold-ing on 'cause I'm tired of grey.__ Are you
born for the mon-ey so I spend it__ quick. Bank says I'm poor but I'm feel-in' rich.__ If you're

© 2012 STELLAR SONGS LTD. and SONY/ATV MUSIC PUBLISHING UK LIMITED
All Rights for STELLAR SONGS LTD. in the U.S. and Canada Controlled and Administered by EMI BLACKWOOD MUSIC INC.
All Rights for SONY/ATV MUSIC PUBLISHING UK LIMITED Administered by SONY/ATV MUSIC PUBLISHING LLC, 8 Music Square West, Nashville, TN 37203
All Rights Reserved   International Copyright Secured   Used by Permission

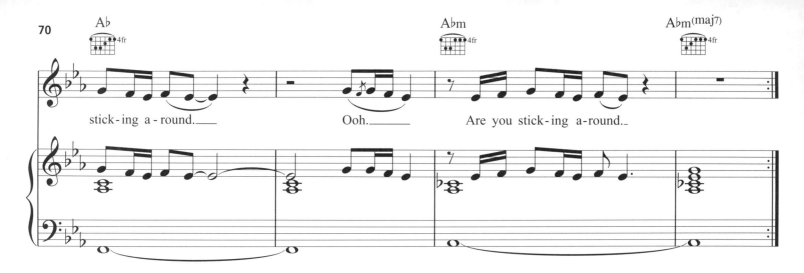

stick-ing a - round.____ Ooh._____ Are you stick-ing a-round._

Hey there,____ hon- ey. You came a- long and stopped_ me____ run - ning.

I'm feel-ing like__ me, back on my__ feet. I'm a ti - ger__ a - gain._____

I'm a ti - ger__ a - gain. 3. Tat-

Hey there,_____ hon - ey. You came a - long and

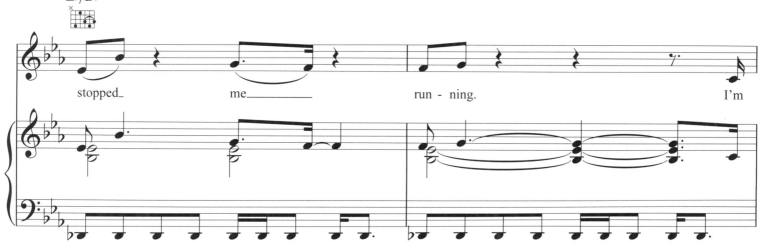

stopped__ me_____ run - ning. I'm

feel - ing like__ me, back on my__ feet. I'm a ti - ger___ a - gain.__

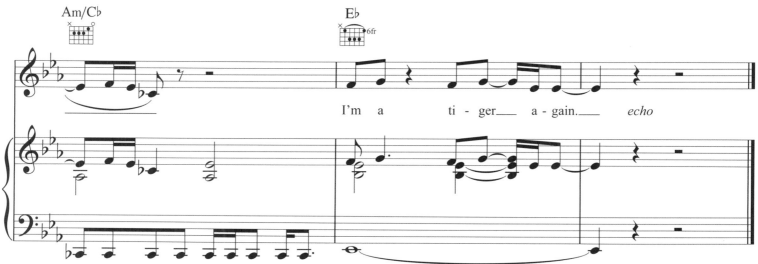

I'm a ti - ger___ a - gain.__ *echo*

# READ ALL ABOUT IT, PART III

Words and Music by EMELI SANDÉ,
TOM BARNES, STEPHEN MANDERSON,
IAIN JAMES, BEN KOHN
and PETER KELLEHER

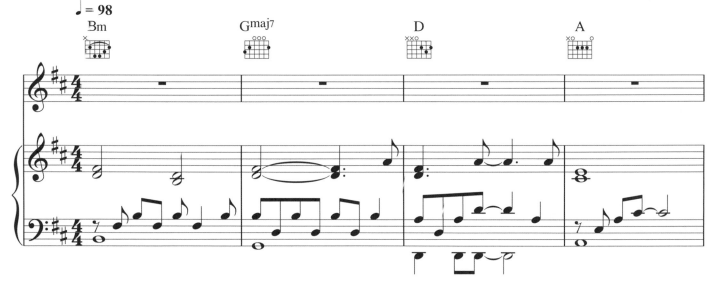

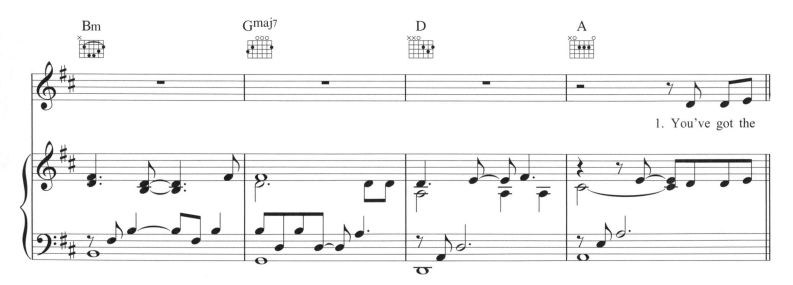

1. You've got the

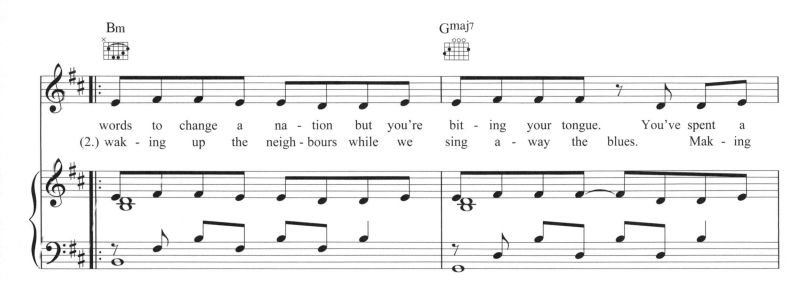

words to change a na-tion but you're bit-ing your tongue. You've spent a
(2.) wak-ing up the neigh-bours while we sing a-way the blues. Mak-ing

© 2012 STELLAR SONGS LTD., SONY/ATV MUSIC PUBLISHING UK LIMITED and BUCKS MUSIC GROUP LTD.
All Rights for STELLAR SONGS LTD. in the U.S. and Canada Controlled and Administered by EMI BLACKWOOD MUSIC INC.
All Rights for SONY/ATV MUSIC PUBLISHING UK LIMITED Administered by SONY/ATV MUSIC PUBLISHING LLC, 8 Music Square West, Nashville, TN 37203
All Rights Reserved   International Copyright Secured   Used by Permission

we're a lit - tle dif - f'rent. There's no need to be a - shamed. You've got the
time we got some air - play of our ver - sion of e - vents. There's no

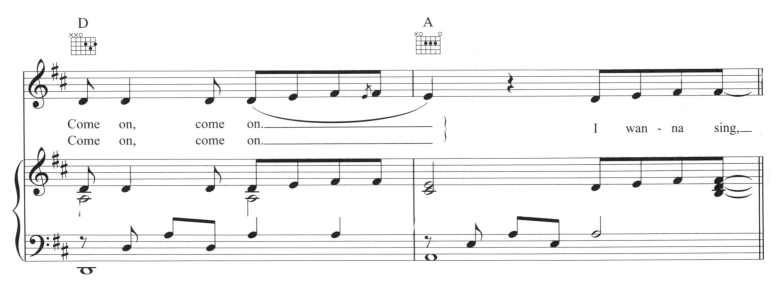

light to fight the shad - ows, so stop hid - ing it a - way.___
need to be a - fraid, I will sing with you my friend.___

Come on, come on._____ I wan - na sing,___
Come on, come on.___

I wan - na shout.___ I wan - na scream___ till the words_ dry out.___

So put in on all____ of the pa - pers. I'm____ not a - fraid.__ They can read__

____ all a - bout__ it. Read____ all a - bout__ it. Oh,____ oh,____ oh,____ oh,__

____ oh. Oh,____ oh,____ oh,_____ oh.____

Oh,____ oh,__ oh,____ oh.____ Oh,__ oh,____ oh,____ oh._____ 2. At night we're

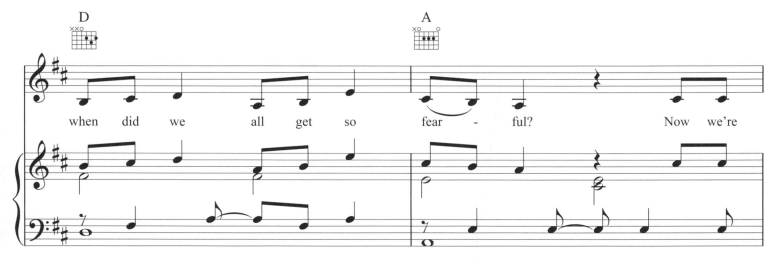

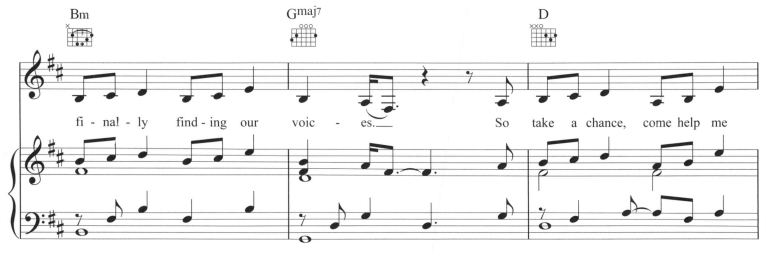

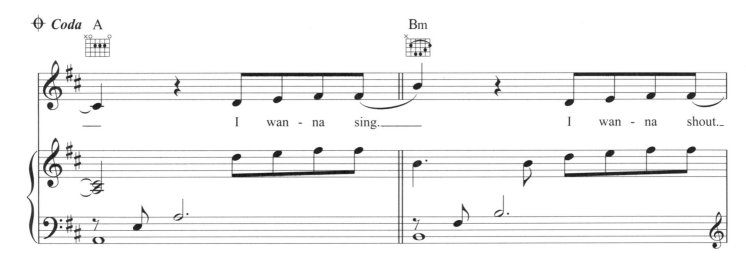

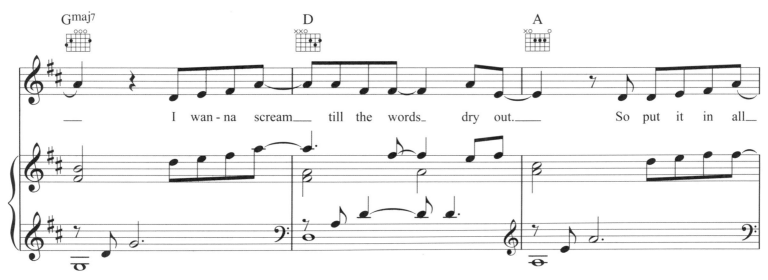

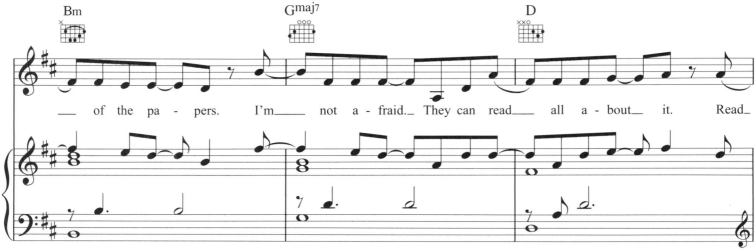